Who Says Women Can't Be DOCTORS?

Who Says Women Can't Be DOCTORS?

The Story of
Elizabeth Blackwell

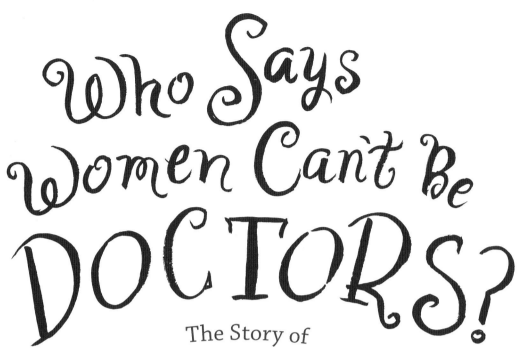

Tanya Lee Stone

Illustrated by
Marjorie Priceman

Christy Ottaviano Books
Henry Holt and Company
New York

Henry Holt and Company, LLC
Publishers since 1866
175 Fifth Avenue
New York, New York 10010
mackids.com

Library of Congress Cataloging-in-Publication Data
Stone, Tanya Lee.
Who says women can't be doctors? : the story of Elizabeth Blackwell /
Tanya Lee Stone ; illustrated by Marjorie Priceman. — 1st ed.
        p.   cm.
Includes bibliographical references.
ISBN 978-0-8050-9048-2 (hc)
1. Blackwell, Elizabeth, 1821–1910. 2. Women physicians—United States—
Biography. I. Priceman, Marjorie, ill. II. Title.
R692.S755 2013   610.92—dc23   [B]   2011043528

First Edition—2013 / Designed by Ashley Halsey
The artist used gouache and india ink on hot-press watercolor paper to create the
illustrations for this book.
Printed in China by Macmillan Production Asia Ltd., Kwun Tong,
Kowloon, Hong Kong (vendor code: 10)

1 3 5 7 9 10 8 6 4 2

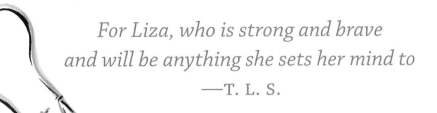

For Liza, who is strong and brave
and will be anything she sets her mind to
—T. L. S.

I'll bet you've met plenty of doctors in your life.
And I'll bet lots of them were women.

Well, you might find this hard to believe, but there once
was a time when girls weren't *allowed* to become doctors.

Back in the 1830s, there were lots of things girls couldn't be. Girls were only supposed to become wives and mothers. Or maybe teachers, or seamstresses.

WOOLEN mill

Being a doctor was definitely not an option.
What do you think changed all that?
Or should I say . . . WHO?

Elizabeth Blackwell, that's who.
A tiny wisp of a girl who wanted to
explore around every corner and
who never walked away from
a challenge.

This was a girl who had once carried her brother over her head until he backed down from their fight.

A girl who tried sleeping on the hard floor with no covers, just to toughen herself up.

A girl who climbed up to her roof and stretched out as far as possible with a spyglass to see what was happening on the other side of town.

But she hadn't always wanted to be a doctor. Actually, blood made her queasy. One time, her teacher used a bull's eyeball to show students how eyes work. Elizabeth was repulsed.

And she hadn't always wanted to help the sick. She had no patience for being sick herself. Whenever she felt ill, she simply went outside for a walk. Once, when she was little, she hid in a closet until she felt better. She hated anyone fussing over her.

So why did she become the first woman doctor? Because one person believed she could and told Elizabeth she was just the kind of smart, determined girl who would change the world.

That person was Mary Donaldson. When Elizabeth was twenty-four, she went to visit her friend who was very ill. Mary told Elizabeth that she would have much preferred being examined by a woman. She urged Elizabeth to consider becoming a doctor.

At first, Elizabeth could not
believe her ears. Even if a girl *could* be a
doctor, why would *she* want to be one?
But Mary's idea gnawed at Elizabeth.
A female doctor.

Elizabeth thought about it the second she got up in the morning.

She thought about it during sewing circles.

She thought about it over tea.

She even dreamed
about it at night.

Finally, Elizabeth asked doctors and friends. Some thought it was a good idea, but didn't think there was any way it could be done. Others said it wasn't right.

women are too weak for such hard work.

women aren't smart enough.

Some people actually laughed at her. They thought she was joking! Elizabeth didn't see *anything* funny about a woman becoming a doctor.

Elizabeth thought it was a fine idea, and her family supported her. She worked as a teacher to earn money and applied to a handful of medical schools. But they all sent back the same answer:

NO.

No women allowed. She tried other schools. More letters arrived at her door. One by one, the answer was always the same.

NO No NO No No No No No No No No No NO no.

Twenty-eight NOs in all.
In different ways, the letters all
said the same thing:
Women *cannot* be doctors.
They *should not* be doctors.

But Elizabeth didn't believe in *couldn't* or *shouldn't*. She refused to give up. She was as stubborn as a mule. Quite rightly!

One day, an envelope arrived from a college. She opened it and everything changed. The answer was . . .

Yes!

Elizabeth packed her bags
for Geneva Medical School
in upstate New York.

The townspeople were expecting her. As she walked down the street, some pointed and stared. They whispered to themselves that she must be wicked—or crazy. Elizabeth thought that at least the students wanted her there. Except they didn't.

The teachers had let the students vote on whether or not to allow Elizabeth to come. And the boys, figuring the school would never really accept a girl, said yes. They planned to turn the whole thing into a big joke.

But the joke was on them!

Their raucous laughter turned to silence as the
ladylike Elizabeth took her seat.
They wondered what kind of girl she was.
The kind of girl who wouldn't take the bait.

Some thought a girl wouldn't be able to keep up.

Except Elizabeth did keep up, often studying past midnight.

Elizabeth proved she was as smart as any boy.

And soon the boys wanted to know what Elizabeth thought about this or that.

It took the townspeople longer to accept her. Some people are afraid of anything new or different.

Not Elizabeth.

On January 23, 1849, Elizabeth graduated . . . with the highest grades in the whole class!

She had become the first woman doctor in America.

Although many people were proud, others were angry. One doctor even wrote, "I hope, for the honor of humanity, that [she] will be the last."

But as you know, she certainly was

Not.

Author's Note

Elizabeth Blackwell was born on February 3, 1821, in Bristol, England. Although it was quite unusual for the time, her father insisted on making sure his daughters were as well educated as his sons. Her family moved to the United States when she was eleven.

After Elizabeth graduated from medical school in 1849, no one would hire her to work as a doctor. She went to England and France to further her training, then moved back to New York City when she was thirty years old. Finally, she persuaded a landlord to rent her office space. She hung out a sign with her name on it: ELIZABETH BLACKWELL, M.D. But the other tenants were horrified and all moved out.

Frustrated, Elizabeth took long walks through the streets of New York City trying to figure out what to do. She saw many poor women and children huddled in doorways and in alleys. They were dirty and in need of care. She decided to hold a free clinic and teach people how staying clean would help them be healthy. Pretty soon, people started to talk about the wonderful new woman doctor in town. Over the years, Elizabeth and her sister Emily, who also became a doctor, healed hundreds of people. In time, they had so many female patients, the sisters started their own hospital. The New York Infirmary for Women and Children, which opened on May 12, 1857, was the first hospital run by women, for women.

In 1868, Elizabeth opened a medical school—just for women—the Women's Medical College of the New York Infirmary. The next year, she moved back to her native England and helped organize the London School of Medicine for Women. And in 1871, she helped start the National Health Society, which focused on educating people about health, hygiene, and the prevention of disease.

Elizabeth never married, but she did adopt a girl who was an orphan. Her name was Kitty Barry.

Elizabeth Blackwell died on May 31, 1910, at the age of eighty-nine. Many schools and hospitals are named in her honor. And, according to the Association of American Medical Colleges, more than half of all U.S. medical school students today are women. This would not have been possible without the courage and determination of this extraordinary woman.

Elizabeth Blackwell, at around sixty-five years old.

Sources Used

Ashby, Ruth, and Deborah Gore Ohrn, eds. *Herstory: Women Who Changed the World*. New York: Viking, 1995.

Blackwell, Elizabeth. *Pioneer Work in Opening the Medical Profession to Women*. New York: Source Book Press, 1970 (reprint of 1895 edition).

Buckmaster, Henrietta. *Women Who Shaped History*. New York: Collier Books, 1966.

Fancourt, Mary St. John. *They Dared to Be Doctors: Elizabeth Blackwell and Elizabeth Garrett Anderson*. London: Longmans, 1965.

Snodgrass, Mary Ellen. *Crossing Barriers: People Who Overcame*. Englewood, CO: Libraries Unlimited, 1993.

Wilson, Dorothy Clarke. *Lone Woman: The Story of Elizabeth Blackwell, the First Woman Doctor*. Boston: Little, Brown, 1970.